# To Love or To Hate

## Book Two

### Ashleigh Henry

If you love someone tell them
because hearts are often broken
by words left unspoken.

Copyright© 2021 by Ashleigh Publishing LLC

All rights reserved. This book or any portion thereof may not be reproduced or used in any manner whatsoever without the express written permission of the publisher except for the use of brief quotations in a book review.

Printed in the United States of America

First Printing, 2021

ISBN 978-0-578-94014-4

For permissions and more information please send emails to info@ashleighpublishingllc.com or vist www.ashleighpublishingllc.com

# Acknowledgements

I must first start by acknowledging God, who is the head of my life, for giving me the inspiration, knowledge, and wisdom to write this book.

I want to take this opportunity to thank my mother, Novlet Shand, for always supporting and telling me that I can do all things through Christ, who strengthens me. She is my rock and my protector since I was born.

She always tells me that there is no limit and no mountain that I cannot climb with Jesus Christ in my life directing my path. I thank God for her because I would not be who I am today without her prayers and unconditional love.

# Table of Contents

Acknowledgements..................................................pg.3

Introduction...........................................................pg.5

Chapter 1: Does Time Heal All Wounds?...................pg.6

Chapter 2: To Rekindle An Old Flame or Burn It.pg.13

Chapter 3: Some Things Are Better Left Unsaid....pg.18

Chapter 4: A Girl's Night Out Gone Wrong.............pg.25

Chapter 5: Except The Unexcpeted..........................pg.42

Chapter 6: A Demand For Sex..................................pg.54

Chapter 7: When It Rains It Pours...........................pg.63

Chapter 8: A Blessing In Disguise............................pg.71

Chapter 9: Who Is The Father of The Child?...........pg.80

Books By The Author................................................pg. 91

About The Author:....................................................pg.93

# Introduction

Victoria has finally learned to love herself for who she is. She has forgiven herself for the mistakes she made in the past. She regrets not telling Amy who her biological father was as a child because her daughter has to deal with harassment and shame at school. Victoria did not realize how much it would affect her daughter. Unfortunately, she has to live with the feeling of guilt and shame from her past decisions. That was exposed and revealed to the public. She cant escape her past, for it has become her reality. She hopes one day Mark will forgive her. Only time can heal all wounds. Due to her promiscuous past, she was threatened by her ex to offer sexual services to keep the custody of her child, or she would go to jail. Should she rekindle that old flame or burn it?

# Chapter One

*Does time heal all wounds?*

A few years have passed, and Victoria has finally learned to love herself for who she is. She has forgiven herself for the mistakes she made in the past. For the first time in her life, she has learned to take full accountability for her actions. She acknowledges that she made some decisions in her life that she is not proud of. However, she wishes she could take it all back. So she can start all over again with Mark, but she can't. She can't change the past, but she can change the future. She hopes one day Mark will forgive her. Only time can heal all wounds. She realized that she couldn't force a man to love her, and she can't force a man to be with her.

# Does Time Heal All Wounds?

If a man loves a woman, he will do anything to be with her. No one would have to force the man to do anything. He will do it freely at his own will. Victoria wants Mark back, but he still does not want to be with her. She is still hurting because she still loves him dearly. She is thorn because she thinks she can't move on without him by her side. He was her king, and she was his queen. She never had a man treat her like the way he did. He was passionate, and he loved her despite her flaws.

He knew she wasn't perfect, but he looked behind her flaws and accepted her for who she was. He knew he couldn't change her past, but he believed in her future. After the breakup, Victoria tried so many times to reach out to him, but he never responded. She called and texted him numerous times, but he did not answer. She believes he blocked her because after a while, her calls went straight to voicemail, and her texts were never delivered. How can I stop loving him?

# Does Time Heal All Wounds?

Victoria said to herself every day; she was so hurt and heartbroken. After all the unanswered calls and texts, she felt rejected. This feeling of brokenness and rejection had finally turned into hate. She hates him for leaving her, but she loves him because he taught her how to love.

On the other hand, she is still upset with Richard, the father of her child. For all the pain he put her through all these years. Every time she looks at her daughter Amy. She sees Richard, and it brings back all the anger she has in her heart for him. Richard was her first love, but Mark has her true love. Now that everyone knows Richard is the father of her child. Victoria regrets not telling Amy who her biological father was as a child because now her daughter has to deal with harassment and shame at school. Victoria did not realize how much it would affect her daughter.

# Does Time Heal All Wounds?

She is ashamed Amy found out this way. She can't imagine how her daughter feels, but she wishes things were different. Since the big news came out, Amy has been rude and rebellious. Amy is hurting, and she is acting out of anger. Unfortunately, Victoria has to live with the feeling of guilt and shame from her past decisions. That was exposed and revealed to the public. She cant escape her past, for it has become her reality, and it is time to face her truth.

(Knock...Knock)

Victoria runs to the front door to see who it is. To her surprise, she saw Richard at the front door. She couldn't believe he was there. She said to herself she didn't have to answer the door because Amy is not there. She waited 10 minutes to see if he would leave, but he didn't. To her curiosity, she opened the door to see why he came to her home.

# Does Time Heal All Wounds?

(Victoria opens the front door)

Hi Vicki, how are you? I'm fine Richard, what are you doing here? Wow, Victoria, that's how you welcome your guest into your home. Shut up, Richard; why are you here? I came to talk to you. I tried calling you, but it went straight to voicemail. What do you want, Richard? We need to talk, Victoria. Can I come in? I don't have time for this, Richard! I have other things to do! Vicki, it's important! Can I please come in?  Fine!

(Victoria steps back and opens the front door wider to let Richard in)

Hi Victoria, how are you? Richard skip the small talk; why are you here? Vicki, I'm so sorry for what my parents did to you and Amy. All these years, I allowed Amy to grow up without a father. I hid this secret from the world. I feel horrible; I'm such a bad person. Please allow me to make things right with you and Amy. Let me finally be the father she deserves to have.

# Does Time Heal All Wounds?

I want to have a relationship with my daughter. Is she here? No, she is at school. Okay, what time will she be home? She will be home soon. Vicki, can I wait here for her?

(Richard puts his hand around Victoria's waist)

Richard, what are you doing? Don't touch me! Aren't you married? I'm sorry, Vicki, but I couldn't help myself; you're so beautiful. I'm still in love with you, and I want us to be a family.

(Richard leans over to kiss Victoria on her lips, but Victoria slaps him across his face)

What's wrong with you, Richard? What are you doing? Are you drunk? Get the hell out of my house! What kind of woman do you think I am? Vicki, everyone knows what kind of woman you are; it's all over the news and social media. You are an escort! It's your job, and I am going to pay you for your services. I don't see what's the big problem.

# Does Time Heal All Wounds?

Get the hell out of my house, Richard, before I call the police! I'm sorry, don't call the police. I sincerely apologize; it was rude of me to do that to you. Victoria, I know I messed up big time, but please let me make it up to you.

(Richard leans towards Victoria to grab her hand)

Please don't touch me, Richard! You are married, and you're trying to have sex with me. Did you even come here to start a relationship with Amy or to have sex with me? Vicki, it's not even like that! I told you I want us to be a family. I know I messed up in the past. I have a lot of explaining to do, but can you please give me a chance to fix it? Richard, having sex with me will not fix it! Vicki, what do you want? I'll give you anything you want; please forgive me.

# Chapter Two

## *To Rekindle An Old Flame Or Burn It*

Vicki, answer me; how can I fix this? I am here, and I want to make things right. I lost years of Amy's childhood not being in her life. When I see you and Amy, it kills me on the inside because she looks just like me. Amy does not deserve to have me as a father; she deserves better. Your damn right, Richard; the only reason you are here is because your dirty laundry was exposed to the world. If it were not revealed, you would not be here. Get the hell out of the house; you are a disgrace to your daughter! You are acting as if you are better than me, Victoria. Look at your past before you judge someone else. Why did you accept the money from my mother to keep my child away from me?

# To Rekindle An Old Flame Or Burn It

Does Amy know what you did to separate her from her father before she was born? What kind of mother are you? Look at what you have become with the millions of dollars my mother gave you. An escort! What a disgrace! How can Amy look up to you as a role model? She has no guidance, and I won't be surprised if she follows in your footsteps in becoming a whore.

(Victoria throws her drink in his face)

What the hell is wrong with you, Vicki? You can't handle the truth, huh? You can diss it, but you can't take it! I am not a disgrace; you are Richard! As a matter of fact, Vicki, I'm going to file for full custody of my daughter. I was not there for Amy in her childhood, but I will recuse her from her misery. You will not take Amy away from me, Richard! Oh yes, I will! Just watch and see Victoria! When the courts find out that you don't have a legitimate job.

# To Rekindle An Old Flame Or Burn It

You are not financially stable, Victoria, and you sell pussy for a living. They will give me full custody of my daughter right away. Richard, get the fuck out of my house! Who the hell do you think you are, taking my child away from me? I am her father, Richard Williams, Amy's biological father. One of the wealthiest black millionaires in Georgia. Please don't act like you don't know who I am! Victoria, you can't afford to take care of Amy. Look at this piece of shit house you live in. You can't afford to do better! I bet you can't afford to get an attorney for the custody trial, either.

(Victoria slaps Richard across the face and pushes him towards the front door)

Just because I won't give you some pussy does not mean you can come into my house and disrespect me! Don't you ever disrespect me again or come back to my house, you piece of shit! Keep it up, Victoria! I can press charges against you for assault.

# To Rekindle An Old Flame Or Burn It

Did you forget my mother is an attorney! I don't care who your mother is; get the hell out of my house before I call the cops! I have a gun here, Richard, and I'm not afraid to use it. Is that a threat, Victoria?

(Richard reaches to grab Victoria's waist again)

Stop touching me, Richard, before I shoot you! Your so aggressive, Vicki, and I like it! It is turning me on!  All you have to do is give me some pussy, and I won't file for custody of Amy! It's that simple, and the choice is yours.

(Victoria kicks Richard in his genital area)

Victoria, that hurts; why would you do that? I was trying to help you find an easier way out, but now you will regret this. I promise you I am coming back with revenge and for full custody of my daughter.

# To Rekindle An Old Flame Or Burn It

(Victoria pushes him out of her house and slaps the door in his face)

I can't believe I opened the door and let him into my house. Richard is still the same, and he has not changed. He must be out of his mind to take Amy away from me. I'm not going down without a fight.

(Victoria paced the floor in her living room back and forth)

Lord, what should I do? My past has caught up to me, and I am fully exposed. I can't afford to get an attorney, and I don't have a legit job. Please don't let Richard take my child away from me. My entire business is on blogs and social media outlets. If we go to court, I can lose full custody of my child.

(Victoria cries to herself as she ponders what to do)

Lord, help me to keep full custody of my child in this custody battle!

# Chapter Three

## *Some Things Are Better Left Unsaid*

(Amy walks in the house from school and sees her mother crying)

Hey Amy, how was school today? It was okay, mom. Why are you crying? Please don't ruin your makeup. You look so pretty, mom. Aww, your so sweet, baby! You always make me happy! You are my sunshine, the joy of my life. I know, mom, but what is wrong? I hate to see you cry. Mom, you are stronger than this. God is bigger than all of your problems. Just leave it to him! Amy, I know God will take care of it eventually. I am not as strong as you think; sometimes, I hurt too. It is hard trying to be strong all the time. Sometimes I need to cry to let it all out!

# Some Things Are Better Left Unsaid

Baby, I want you to know that I love you so much, and no matter where life takes us. I will always be there for you. I will always support you in everything that you do. Mom, please tell me what is wrong? You are starting to scare me! Amy, I don't know how to say this to you, but you need to know! I feel so ashamed and heartbroken to tell you this. What is it, mom? Just say it, please! I am getting very anxious! What could it be? I already know who my father is, and I know you are an escort from the blogs! Please tell me, how can it be worse than this? How do you know I am an escort, Amy? Mom, it's all over the blogs.

Everyone knows, cmon how could you think I would not find out, and how dumb do you think I am? I am sorry, Amy, but it is hard for me to tell you this. Yes, I am an escort, and I always knew who your father was all these years. Your father and I were high school sweethearts. He was my first boyfriend. We loved each other dearly back then.

# Some Things Are Better Left Unsaid

However, I got pregnant in my last year of high school, and your grandmother, who is your father's mother, did not want me to give birth to you. She wanted me to have an abortion, and I refused to do so. She pressured me to sign an agreement. She bridged me with money! The agreement stated if I gave birth to her son's child. I should keep you away from your father, and I should not have a relationship and no communication with him. I signed that letter to help us financially. I did not have any money at the time to take care of us!

Yes, I regretted signing that agreement because I wanted your father in our lives. However, your grandmother would put me in jail if I broke that agreement. So, what happens now, mom? You broke that agreement! Are you going to jail? I don't know, Amy. Why would you sign that, mom? Are you stupid? I can't trust you with my life! All you had to do was get a job to support us financially, but you wanted an easier way out.

# Some Things Are Better Left Unsaid

You probably did not know your mistakes would come back to bite you like it is now. Only God knows what you would do for money? I can't believe you would do this to me? What were you thinking? I can't look at you the same as my respectful and dignified mother. Everyone at school knows our business and makes fun of me since the news came out. The kids at school call you a whore. They asked me how much do you charge for your services. I am embarrassed and ashamed of you! I don't want you to attend any of my parent-teacher conferences or any events at school.

I get bullied constantly because of you! I always knew you had many boyfriends, but I never knew you were selling pussy all these years. Now I understand why Mark broke up with you. Which man would want to marry a whore!

# Some Things Are Better Left Unsaid

(Victoria slaps Amy across the face)

That is enough, Amy; you will not disrespect me! I am your mother; show me some respect! I am 16 years old, and I am not a child. I am a teenager. I can speak to you as I feel. Do you want me to tell you lies? I am telling you the truth!

(Victoria slaps Amy in the face again)

You will not disrespect me in my house! Do you hear me? Well, I am moving out! Where are you moving to, Amy? You don't have a job! Where is the money my grandmother gave you? I want it! I can buy my own house with that money! How much money did my grandmother give you? I don't remember Amy, and that is none of your business! Do you even know what you have put me through, Mom? I almost watched you commit suicide! How does a child recover from that?

# Some Things Are Better Left Unsaid

I am so sorry, Amy! I don't think you are sorry, mom. You should be ashamed! If you were sorry, you would not be kicking me out of the house, and you would not sell me for money! What kind of mother are you?

(Amy starts to cry)

How can you do this to me? Do I even mean anything to you? Were you using me to be a part of your get-rich-quick scheme? I am so heartbroken, and I feel so unwanted. Amy, it is not like that! Please don't take it that way! I love you so much, but I had to make some decisions when I was younger to survive. So we would not struggle. I was poor, and I did not have anyone to help me financially. I don't want to hear your sob story, mom! I still deserved better. I can't even look at you! You let me down! I always routed for you to become better. You were my idol, but not anymore.

# Some Things Are Better Left Unsaid

Amy, I am so sorry, and I promise I will make it up to you! Mom, you can't erase the past, so you cant make it up to me.

(Victoria reaches to hug Amy, but Amy pushes her away)

      Please give me some space.

(Amy walks upstairs to her room with tears in her eyes)

Amy, I love you so much; please don't turn your back on me when I need you the most. I will give you some alone time to think but remember. I will always be here for you no matter what happens, because I am your mother.

# Chapter Four

## *A Girl's Night Out Gone Wrong*

(Victoria walks into the kitchen and opens a bottle of wine to relieve her stress)

I don't know how to fix this, and I cant tell Amy her father is filing for full custody of her. She would call him and ask him to pick her up right away. I will not let that happen. He will not take my child away from me. I have to find a way to fix this problem before it gets worse. If I have to sleep with this man to keep my child, unfortunately, I have to. I will do anything to keep full custody of my daughter.

(Victoria calls Dina)

Hello... Hi, Dina, it's me, Vicki. I am so stressed I need a girl's night out! Is everything okay, Vicki?

# A Girl's Night Out Gone Wrong

I will tell you all about it later. Now is not the time to talk about it in detail. Okay, I understand, Vicki. I will be at your house in an hour to pick you up! Okay, Thank you, Dina!

(Victoria runs upstairs to get ready)

Beep Beep! Wow, that was quick. Dina is here already. Time went by so quickly!

(Victoria knocks on Amy's door)

Amy, I will be right back; I am going out with Dina.

(Amy opens the door)

Can she drop me off at grandma's house? Of course, she can! Are you okay? I need time to think away from you, mom. I understand, Amy! I told you a lot all at once, but you needed to know. Thank you for telling me, mom; at least this information came from your mouth.

# A Girl's Night Out Gone Wrong

Okay, smart mouth Amy! I already called grandma; she knows I am coming. I am already packed and ready to go. Can we leave now, mom? How long will you be staying at grandma's house, Amy? I don't know yet; mom, I need time to think away from you, as I said before.

(Victoria and Amy walks downstairs towards the front door into Dina's car)

Hey, Amy how are you? I could be better, Dina! Are you okay, Amy? I don't want to talk about it right now! Can you bring me to my grandmother's house, please? Of course, Amy!

(Dina drives her car to Victoria's mother's house)

Victoria, you look beautiful as always. Thank you, Dina!

(Dina turns up the music in the car to ease the tension between Victoria and Amy)

# A Girl's Night Out Gone Wrong

Thank God we are finally here, Dina. The tension in this car was going to kill me.

(Amy comes out of the car and slaps the car door)

Vicki, what is wrong with Amy? I told her everything, and she is having a hard time accepting it. Oh, that makes sense! I apologize; she slapped your car door out of anger towards me. It's okay, Vicki, I understand. I will be right back, Dina. I am going to walk Amy to the front door.

(Victoria comes out of the car and walks over to Amy)

How long will you be staying here? I don't know, mom!

(Victoria's mom opens the front door)

Hi grandma!

# A Girl's Night Out Gone Wrong

(Amy runs to hug her grandmother)

Hi baby! Is everything alright, sweetheart? No, grandma, we have a lot to talk about it. Okay, sweetheart, go inside so I can speak to your mother. Victoria, what is going on? Why are you dressed like a whore! This is not a good look, especially when everyone knows your business from the blogs. Mom, I am stressed out! I need to go out and have a drink! Victoria, you need God; please go back to church! God can fix this situation! Victoria, I am assuming Amy knows everything. Yes, she deserves to know, mom. The truth was going to come out sooner or later.

Victoria, it is time you act like a mother! Stop leaving Amy here when things get tough. You can't run away from your problems, Victoria! I'm not running away, mom. I am going out with Dina for drinks. I asked Amy how long will she be staying here, and she said she doesn't know. Victoria, you are the parent; you can't let Amy run things. You have to put your foot down!

# A Girl's Night Out Gone Wrong

You are the parent, and she is the child! You are right, mom; something else happened, and it is stressing me out! I have to get a drink to relieve my stress; what is it, Vicki? I can't talk about it right now. I will tell you about it another time. As for now, please take care of my daughter for me until things get better. Okay, Vicki, no problem! Have a good night, mom! Goodnight Vicki!

(Victoria walks towards Dina's car)

Girl, let's get drunk tonight! I need it! If you only knew what I am going through right now! Vicki, please tell me all about it!

(Victoria tells Dina all that happened last night with Richard. While she drives to a nightclub)

OMG! What a surprise! I thought we were having drinks tonight at a restaurant, Dina. No, Vicki, you seem down. I want to cheer you up! That's why we are here!

# A Girl's Night Out Gone Wrong

(They walk into the nightclub together)

Wow, Vicki, everyone is looking at you! You look incredibly gorgeous tonight! Thank you, love! Let's get our drinks and get this party started!

(As Victoria looks across the bar she saw Richard staring at her)

Why does he have to be here? Who are you talking about, Vicki? I wanted to go out and have a fun night instead of worrying about my problems. Richard is here, Dina! Are you talking about Richard, your baby daddy? Yes, he is here, and he is staring at me from across the bar. Oh lord! Vicki, do you want to leave? No, I am not leaving! I will not let him ruin my night! Okay, don't worry, girl, I am here with you. You are not by yourself. Let's take a shot and say fuck him! Yes, Dina, now you are speaking my language.

# A Girl's Night Out Gone Wrong

(Victoria and Dina take eight shots of Hennessy back to back)

Omg Dina, I am so drunk! This is the best girl's night ever!

(Victoria and Dina dance the night away on the dancefloor)

Dina, my feet are hurting! Okay, Vicki, find us a seat. I am going to the bathroom.

(Dina walks to the bathroom as Victoria takes a seat in the VIP section of the nightclub)

I am so glad I can finally take off my heels and rest my feet.

(To her surprise, she sees Richard walking over to her VIP section)

Hey there beautiful! What do you want, Richard? I wanted to check on you to see if you're okay. I am great, Richard! Now you can leave! Vicki that is no way to speak to me.

# A Girl's Night Out Gone Wrong

(Victoria rolls her eyes as Richard takes a seat next to her)

Baby girl, you have to show me respect; you know who I am and what I can do! Do not take me lightly!

(Richard bites his lower lip as he stares at Victoria)

You look so beautiful tonight! If you only knew the thoughts that are going through my head right now!

(Richard reaches to touch Victoria's legs, but she pushes him away)

Please don't touch me, Richard, go home to your wife! I don't want to go home to my wife, Vicki. I want to stay here with you! My feelings for you have never changed, and I can't get over you no matter what I do! I have been running away from the truth for far too long. It is time for me to confess I am still in love with you, and I want you to be mine.

# A Girl's Night Out Gone Wrong

Richard, have you been drinking? Yes, I have, but I believe it is destiny that you and I are here tonight. It is not by chance, and I won't miss this opportunity to tell you that I love you!

(Richard slowly caress Victoria's thigh as he tries to kiss her, and they both lean in for a kiss)

What is going on here, Richard? Are you trying to kiss my friend?

(Richard and Victoria were surprised, Dina walked into the VIP section of the nightclub unexpectedly)

Hi Dina, is that a problem if I kiss your friend? Yes, you are a married man! Are you okay Victoria, is Richard bothering you? Actually, he was just leaving Dina. Sweetheart, are you sure you want me to leave? Our night was just getting started! Yes, I am sure, Richard! Dina, have you paid your mortgage this month? Why would you ask me that?

# A Girl's Night Out Gone Wrong

I know your house is going into foreclosure, and you need to pay $12,000 to stop it. How do you know that, Richard? Don't worry about how I know. Here is my proposition for you, I will give you $12,000 to pay for your home. So you can leave Victoria and I alone for the night. In my eyes, it's a win for both of us! So what's your decision, Dina? Vicki, will you be okay if I leave you here alone with Richard? I need to pay my mortgage before my house goes into foreclosure. Yes, I am a grown woman. I can take care of myself! Take his money and pay for your mortgage, Dina. Thank you, Vicki!

(Dina takes the money and walks out of the nightclub)

Now that I have you alone, Vicki, I want to give you all the love that you have been missing from me all these years. Let me show you how I feel about you!

# A Girl's Night Out Gone Wrong

(Richard passionately kisses Victoria and slowly runs his hand along the top of her leg towards her inner thigh)

Let's leave this nightclub together and go to my penthouse. I want to treat you like the queen you deserve to be! Richard, you are a married man. I can't have sex with you! I will leave my wife for you, Vicki! You are the woman that I always wanted to be with all these years! I don't want to mess it up! Please give me a chance to make it up to you. So we can be the family I always wanted.

Just the three of us, you, Amy, and I. Isn't that what you always wanted, Vicki? Yes, Richard, I always wanted us to be a family. Then come with me tonight, sweetheart. I promise you won't regret it. You are very persuasive, Richard, but you are a married man. Vicki, as I said before, I will leave my wife for you. Vicki, what else can I do to convince you? I want you so bad, and I am willing to do anything to have you tonight in my bed.

# A Girl's Night Out Gone Wrong

Well, there is something you can do for me. What is it, sweetheart? I will give you anything you want. Don't file for custody of Amy, and I will spend the night with you. That sounds like a plan, sweetheart! Let's leave this nightclub now and make my dreams come to reality!

(Richard and Victoria leave the nightclub together)

Vicki, I cant wait to see what the night has in store for us. Let us see what happens, Richard. The night is still young.

(They wait outside the nightclub as the valet driver gets Richard's car)

Vicki, are you cold? Yes, Richard, it is chilly. I don't have a coat with me, but my body can keep you warm.

(Richard hugs Vicki from behind to keep her warm)

# A Girl's Night Out Gone Wrong

Wow, Richard, you are a slick guy. How long have you been waiting to touch my body? All night, sweetheart, to be honest!

(The valet driver parks Richard's red corvette in front of Victoria)

Is this your car Richard? Yes, it is, sweetheart.

(Richard opens the car door for Victoria)

Go inside and have a seat, beautiful! Thank you, Richard; you are such a gentleman tonight. I will do anything for you, sweetheart.

(Richard drives Victoria to his penthouse)

Wow! You have such a lovely place, Richard! Thank you, sweetheart. Where is your wife? She is at home, Vicki. Does she know you have a penthouse? No, she does not know that I have a penthouse. Don't worry; she won't come here unexpectedly. How often do you cheat on your wife, Richard?

# A Girl's Night Out Gone Wrong

Why would you ask me that, Vicki? You don't look like a man that is nervous about cheating on his wife! Well, Vicki, I have cheated on my wife before. To be honest, I don't love my wife. I care for her, but I don't love her. I was forced to marry her by my parents; it was an arranged marriage for power, wealth, and respect. Are you serious, Richard? Yes, I am! As I said before, you are the woman I have been in love with all these years, and I'm not going to mess up this opportunity. You are the woman I want! Enough talking, Victoria. It's time for me to show you how I feel about you.

(Richard passionately kisses Victoria and zips down her dress with his teeth)

Richard, you are a man of many talents!

(Richard was sexually aroused as Victoria stepped out of her dress naked)

My God, you are so sexy! Where are your undergarments, Vicki? I didn't wear any tonight.

# A Girl's Night Out Gone Wrong

(Richard quickly grabs Victoria and picks her up)

Victoria, you don't know how long I was waiting for this!

Richard throws her on his bed, and he starts to make love to her. The louder she moaned, the harder he would penetrate her. He inserted every inch of his penis inside of her without considering her comfort. At first, the sex was enjoyable for her, but she could not handle it after a while. Richard was not gentle with her. He was very rough. Richard had a bigger penis than she thought. It was 12 inches, to be exact. She had to be quiet and bear the pain of every stroke. She felt so useless as she laid on her back, waiting for it to be over.

She felt so uncomfortable, but all she could think about was Amy. She grabbed the sheets of his bed to handle his embrace. Victoria stared at the ceiling of his bedroom, waiting for Richard to climax.

# A Girl's Night Out Gone Wrong

She felt so ashamed, and she couldn't believe she had sex with Richard, but she willing to do anything to keep full custody of her daughter. When he finally climaxed, they both laid in his bed naked together. He held Victoria in his arms as he told her he loved her. He told her she could stay the night and that he did not want to lose her.

# Chapter Five

*Except The Unexcepted*

The following morning Victoria wakes up to the smell of freshly made pancakes, bacon, eggs, and sausage. Richard prepared a plate of food for her. So she could have breakfast in bed. Vicki, last night was incredible, and I didn't want it to end. I am happy you are here with me.
Aww, your so sweet, Richard. Thank you for breakfast. I appreciate it. Can you sleep over tonight, Vicki? I'm sorry, Richard, but I can't sleep over tonight, maybe another time. I already have other plans. I hope you're not seeing another guy tonight. No, Richard, I am a mother, and I have to stay home with Amy. Of course, our daughter comes first.

# Except The Unexcepted

I understand; maybe I can come over, and we can spend quality time together as a family. Richard, let's take it slow and not rush into things. I understand you want to build a relationship with Amy. Let me talk to our daughter first to see if she is ready to talk to you. Okay, Vicki, you know Amy better than I do. I can't wait to see her. She looks just like me. Yes, she does!

(Victoria phone rings)

Sweetheart, your phone is ringing; it could be Amy. I should answer it! So she can hear the sound of her father's voice. Don't answer my phone, Richard!. Don't be so clingy! I can answer my phone myself!

(Richard hands the phone to Victoria)

Okay, Mrs bossy, I like it when you are aggressive.

(Victoria looks at the caller ID, and she sees Mark calling her)

# Except The Unexcepted

Who is calling you Vicki? I don't know Richard. I am not going to answer it. Whoever is calling can leave a message.

(Richard grabs Victoria by her waist)

How about we go for round two before I go to work?

No, Richard, I have to go home to Amy. Okay, sweetheart, can I bring you home? No, I already arranged for a uber driver to pick me up. Okay, sweetheart, when can I see you again? I will let you know, Richard.

(Beep! Beep!)

That must be my uber driver outside waiting for me.

(Richard kisses Victoria as she leaves his penthouse, and he watches her walk away)

# Except The Unexcepted

Damn! I can't believe that ass is mine. Richard, I never said I was yours. I only gave myself to you for one night to keep full custody of our daughter; that was our arrangement you agreed to last night. Remember that!

(Victoria goes into the uber and waves goodbye to Richard)

Omg! I can't believe Mark called me! I wonder why he called, but he did not leave a message. I am curious, did he call me by mistake? I am going to call him to find out.

(Victoria calls Mark in the uber)

Hello... Hi Mark, this is Victoria; you called me earlier. I hope everything is okay with you? I am so glad to hear your voice, Victoria. I have missed you so much. I have longed to listen to your voice. I apologize for blocking your calls and texts; I was upset with you. I blocked you because I was hurting, and I did not know how to deal with the pain.

# Except The Unexcepted

The distance is killing me, and I needed to hear your voice; that is why I called you. Mark, I missed you too, and I apologize for hurting you; that was never my intention. Victoria, can I see you tonight? I thought you were engaged. I am, but I am willing to break up with my fiancé for you. I don't love her as much as I love you. The love I have for you is different, and I don't want to lose it. Mark, you blocked me for a very long time. I thought you were entirely over me. I thought you hated me. No, I don't hate you, Victoria. I am in love with you, and I want to marry you!

I want to take the engagement ring off from my fiancé and give it to you. You are the woman I want. You are the woman I want to spend the rest of my life with. You are the woman I can't live without. You are the one, Victoria. I don't care about what you did in the past. I don't care about what people say about you. As long as I have you as my wife, that's all that matters. Omg, Mark, I am completely blown away. Victoria, where are you now? I want to see you.

# Except The Unexcepted

I am in a uber going home. Victoria, I will be at your house in the next 30 minutes. Okay, Mark, I should be home by then. I love you, Victoria. I love you too, Mark.

(Victoria hangs up the phone)

Today must be my lucky day. My prayers were finally answered.

(Victoria pays the uber driver and walks into her home)

Thank God I am home now. I can take a quick shower before my future husband arrives.

(Victoria runs upstairs into the bathroom to take a shower)

When she comes out of the bathroom, she hears someone ringing her doorbell. To her surprise, it was Mark at her front door. Omg, I am not even dressed. She runs into the bathroom and brushes her teeth.

# Except The Unexcepted

She sprays her favorite perfume on herself and runs to the front door.

(Victoria opens the front door to Mark in a wet towel naked)

Hi beautiful!

(Mark gives Victoria a bouquet of red roses)

Aww, your so sweet thank you, love. You're welcome beautiful!

(Victoria invites Mark into her home)

I did not expect to see you in a towel. I just came out of the shower. Would you like a glass of champagne? Yes, Victoria, I would love to!

(Victoria walks into the kitchen and puts her roses in a vase. Then she pours a bottle of champagne into a glass for Mark.)

I am so happy to see you, Victoria! I meant what I said on the phone earlier.

# Except The Unexcepted

I am going to leave my finance for you. Are you serious, Mark? Yes, Victoria, I am! I will break up with her today to prove it to you. Victoria, I want you back, and I am serious. I will never let you go again. I was foolish to let go the love of my life.

(Mark grabs Victoria by her waist and kisses her on her neck)

I know you missed me, Victoria!

(He slides his hands down from her waist and squeezes her ass)

I know you still want me, Victoria! Yes, I am still in love with you, Mark, but I want to do this the right way.

(Mark stares into her eyes and bites his lips)

If you want me to become your wife, go break up with your fiancé first. Victoria, you are turning me on just by standing in this wet towel naked.

# Except The Unexcepted

I can't keep my hands off of you. How do you expect me to stay focus? Are you sure you don't want to kiss and make up first? No, Mark, I am serious! I don't want to get hurt again. I understand, Victoria. I will never hurt you again, I promise.

Mark kisses Victoria on her neck as he caresses her body. Victoria drops her towel to have sex with Mark. She jumps on him and wraps her legs around him. He begins to suck on her nipples in a circular motion with his tongue until they became hard. Then he gently laid her down on the island in the middle of the kitchen as he fingered her clitoris with his tongue. Victoria's moans get louder as her toes began to curl up from her orgasm. Mark picks her up and brings her into the bedroom. He gently lays her down across the bed as he puts her body in various positions to penetrate her. Victoria continues to moan louder and louder as they both climaxed together.

# Except The Unexcepted

Omg, Mark, why do you make love to me so good? I missed you, Victoria; you deserved it!

(They both lay in the bed together staring at each other as they have pillow talk)

Victoria, I hate to leave you like this, but I have to go and break up with my fiancé. I have to prove to you that I am serious about making you, my future wife. I love you, and I will do anything for you.

(Mark puts on his clothes and kisses Victoria)

Don't worry, Victoria, I won't break your heart again. I love you, and you are the apple of my eye. I can't imagine my life without you.

(Mark leaves her home)

What a day! He made love to me so good! I can't even think straight, but I have to focus. Why did this happen to me? Two of the men I have loved my entire life have come back into my life at the same time.

# Except The Unexcepted

Richard wants to leave his wife for me, and Mark will break up with his fiancé for me. I never thought this would ever happen to me. I should be happy, but I am sad. Eventually, I have to choose between Mark and Richard. If I pick Mark, Richard will take my child away from me. If I pick Richard, Mark will hate me forever, and I will lose the opportunity of becoming his wife. I don't know what to do. Richard does not seem like he wants to stop fucking me. He didn't want me to leave his penthouse this morning. He is already clingy. As a matter of fact, he wanted to come over tonight.

I should be happy, but I feel horrible. This day can't get any worse. Eventually, I have to tell Mark the truth so our future relationship can last. However, I want to give Amy the family she deserves, but not like this Richard is a married man. It will not work out between us. I do not want him to leave his wife for me. I want to be with Mark, and I hope Richard does not use our arrangement to his advantage to threaten me.

# Except The Unexcepted

I should give him a written agreement to sign, so he can't deny the arrangement we made. So I keep custody of our child.

# Chapter Six

## *A Demand For Sex*
(Ding...Dong)

Victoria goes to the front door to see who came to her home. To her surprise, it was Mark. She opened the door in excitement to see him. Hey, beautiful, I wanted to come here and ask you face to face and not over the phone.

(Victoria gets anxious)

Okay, Mark, what is it? I broke up with my fiancé, and here is the ring.

(Mark gets down on his knee and proposes to Victoria)

Omg, Mark! What are you doing? Victoria, will you marry me? Yes, I will!

# A Demand For Sex

(Victoria and Mark hug each other in excitement for their engagement)

Victoria, I know you wanted an extravagant proposal, but I did not want to wait. I want you to know I am serious about marrying you. I do not want to hurt you again. I meant what I said to you before, and I had to prove it to you with my actions. Omg, Mark, I don't know what to say! I can't believe this happened. I am happy and honored you chose me to be your wife.

(Victoria starts to cry, and Mark wipes her tears)

Victoria, don't cry. I want to make you happy! I want to spend the rest of my life with you! I proposed to you so quickly because I don't want to waste any time. We are getting older, and I don't want to regret not marrying the woman I love. You can start the wedding planning process as soon as you are ready.

# A Demand For Sex

As I said before, I know this is not an extravagant proposal, but I promise I will make it up to you. I would love to stay and celebrate our engagement, but I have to go to work. I love you, Victoria, have a goodnight!

(Mark kisses Victoria and leaves her home)

Who knew I was so blessed! I am going to be a wife! I never knew this day would come, but I am glad it did! God, you are blessing me, but I don't deserve it.  I want to thank you! I can't believe I will be a doctor's wife soon. I have to get my life in order and tell Richard it is over between us. I will not allow him to mess up my life. Thank God he is the only man I have slept with since Mark and I broke up. Thank God I quit my escorting job as well.  I can't wait to call my mom and tell her the good news she will be so happy. However, I have to call Richard first to straighten out our arrangement.

# A Demand For Sex

(Victoria calls Richard)

Hey, Sexy!.. Hi Richard, how are you? I was thinking about you while I was masturbating, but it would be better if you were here with me. So we can climax together with your sexy ass! OMG, Richard, you are so grouse! Masturbate to your wife and not me! I already told you, Vicki, that I am not in love with her. I am in love with you! Why are you so turned off by me today?

Yesterday, you were moaning my name so loud my neighbors heard everything, and they know I was fucking the shit out of you! Shut up, Richard! I didn't call you to talk about sex! Then what is it, Vicki, because I want to fuck you right now! OMG, Richard, everything is not always about sex! I called you Richard to tell you that Mark and I are back together. We are engaged, and I don't want to have any sexual relations with you. I want to make sure you understood our arrangement. I will not have sex with you again, and I will keep full custody of our daughter. Am I clear, Richard?

# A Demand For Sex

(There is a silence on the phone)

Richard, are you there? Yes, I am here. Did you hear what I said, Richard? I heard what you said, but I did not agree to any arrangement with you! Is there any written proof that was signed between us? I don't think so! So you are still entitled to fuck me whenever I want! I don't care if you are engaged to Mark; you are still mine! Whenever I call, text, or arrive at your home, you are to fuck me on command. Unless you want me to file for custody of our daughter because I can do that.

You know I will win the custody trial, and when I do. I will make sure you have no visiting rights to see our daughter. I will make sure she hates you as much as you poisoned her to hate me! Victoria, I advise you to make the best decision for your child and not for your happiness because I can ruin your entire life. I can also have my mother press charges against you, and you could be locked up in jail for a very long time!

# A Demand For Sex

Would you rather be in a jail cell or in my bed with your legs wide open every night taking this 12-inch dick? The decision is yours, Victoria! Choose wisely! Victoria, are you there? Yes, I am Richard. What is your decision? I will not fuck you again, Richard! I am not your whore! Yes, you are Victoria! You were an escort for many years. This should be easy for you. You use to sell your pussy and open your legs to different men every night! What is the difference now? Remember you are doing this for Amy!

If you love your daughter, you will continue to fuck me! Be smart, Victoria, because you belong to me; I own you now! Now get your ass over here so I can fuck the shit of you! Who the hell do you think you are talking to me like that? I will not allow you to disrespect me! I was stupid to have sex with you to keep custody of my child, and I never do it again. Don't you ever call my phone or come to my home! Leave me the hell alone, Richard! Victoria, you will regret this!

# A Demand For Sex

(Victoria hangs up the phone on Richard)

I can't believe this asshole is threatening me! I have to find a way to beat him at his own game! Damn, I wish my pussy was not so good because I would not be in this situation.

(Victoria kneels down on the floor in her living room as she prays to God)

Lord, I need your help in this situation! I have to tell Mark everything, but I don't know how to! I don't want to break his heart, but I have to tell him the truth! I don't want him to leave me. Amen!

(Victoria calls her mother)

Hello... Hi Mom! Hi Victoria, how are you? I am stressed! I thought your girl's night would relieve your stress, Victoria? Mom, I have good and bad news! Victoria, tell me the good news first. I am engaged, Mark proposed to me!

# A Demand For Sex

Congratulations, Victoria I am so happy for you! Good things come to those that wait, but Victoria, what is the bad news? Richard wants to file for full custody of Amy. What? Yes, mom! If he goes to trial, he will win the case, and I lose custody of my daughter. Victoria, only God can fix this! Mom, it gets worse! I had sex with him the night I went out with Dina for drinks. I told him I would have sex with him to keep full custody of our daughter, and he agreed at that time. However, I told him I am engaged, and I do not want to continue to have sex with him anymore, and he threatened me.

Saying he will file for full custody of Amy, and he will have his mother put me in jail! Are you serious, Victoria? Yes, I am mom, and I don't know what to do! I want to change my life because I am going to a wife. Victoria, you have to tell Mark everything; remember you are engaged now, and he has to know before this situation escalates. Did you have sex with Richard after the engagement?

# A Demand For Sex

No, I had sex with him before Mark, and I started talking again. After I had sex with Richard, that's when Mark called me while I was at Richard's penthouse. What? I thought Mark blocked you, Victoria. Yes, he did, mom, but he unblocked me. Apparently, he missed me, and he wanted me back. Wow, Victoria, look how the devil works, and now you are stuck in a trap! Mom, I should be happy that I am engaged, but I am depressed.

Victoria, come to church with me tomorrow; as I said before, only God can fix this! Okay, mom, I will! How is Amy? She is okay, but she misses you. I miss her too! Is she awake? No, she is sleeping. I will see her tomorrow at church. Mom, I love my daughter, and I do not want to lose her. I know Victoria! I am going to pray for you tonight. Thank you, mom. Have a good night, Victoria! Good night mom!

# Chapter Seven

## *When It Rains It Pours*

The following day Victoria gets up bright and early to go to church with her mother and daughter. She is very excited because she is excepting a blessing by attending church this morning.

(She leaves her home and drives to her mother's house)

(When she arrives, she's seen her daughter and mother outside dressed in their formal attire)

(Victoria walks out of the car and greets them)

Mommy, I missed you so much! I am glad to see you! I am sorry for the way I treated you.

# When It Rains It Pours

You did not deserve it, and I realize it wasn't your fault. You were only protecting me as my mother. Aww, Amy, I missed you, and I love you so much. Thank you for having an understanding heart.

(They walked back to Victoria's car together, then she drove them to church)

When they arrived, they took a seat and participated in praise and worship. While singing, Victoria shed a tear because the words of the songs touched her heart. When the pastor finished his sermon, he asked if anyone in the congregation wanted prayer. Victoria walked up to the altar, and she told the pastor she wanted to change her life. He prayed for her, and she cried. After the prayer, her mother Sarah walked up to the altar and hugged her. They walked back to their seats together, and Victoria's mom told her she was proud of her.

# When It Rains It Pours

(After the service ended, they drove back to Victoria's mom house for Sunday dinner)

Mom, I am so happy I went to church today I feel so relieved and stress-free. I am glad you came with us, Victoria!

(Sarah cooked dinner while Victoria and Amy prepared the dinner table)

To their surprise, the doorbell rang. Mom, are you excepting anyone for dinner? No, I am not Victoria. Can you get the door for me? My hands are full in the kitchen. No problem, mom!

(Victoria walks over to the front door and opens it for their uninvited guest)

To her surprise, she saw Richards's mom Veronica with a stack of papers in her hand with police officers standing behind her. Mom, come here now!

(Amy holds Victoria's hand)

# When It Rains It Pours

Mommy, what is wrong? Who is that? Hi Victoria, it is nice to see you again! I hope all is well with you! I see you have my granddaughter with you! Sweetheart, is she abusing you? Mommy, who is this? Amy, this is your grandmother Veronica. She is your father's mother. Victoria, I hate to arrest you in front of your child. Arrest me for what? What have I done, Veronica? Victoria, don't play stupid you broke our contract, and you assaulted my son! What did you think would happen? There is a breach in our contract! You can't afford to pay me back for the lawsuit I have filed against you. So you will do time in prison! I am glad my granddaughter is here because my son will be filing for full custody of his daughter. Grandma, come here now!

(Sarah drops the pots in the kitchen and runs to the front door)

I have a court order that states Richard will have temporary custody of Amy while you are in jail.

# When It Rains It Pours

(The officers slowly approached Victoria)

Madam, we have a warrant for your arrest for prostitution, sex trafficking, fraud, unlawful possession of a firearm, aggravated assault, and battery. You have the right to remain silent. If you do say anything, what you say can be used against you in a court of law. You have the right to consult with an attorney and have that attorney present during any questioning. If you cannot afford an attorney, one will be appointed for you if you so desire. Madam, please put her hands behind your back.

(Victoria sheds a tear)

Officers, wait! There has to be something we can do to stop this! My daughter is innocent, I swear! Sarah, your daughter will be in prison for a very long time. She will have to plead guilty because she had no representation and no proof. Say goodbye to her daughter because the next time you see her, it will be behind bars.

# When It Rains It Pours

(Veronica laughs while the officers handcuff Victoria in front of her child and mother)

Madam, for the time being, your child will be in temporary custody with her father while you are in prison. Amy yells, leave my mother alone! She is not a criminal, and I am not going anywhere with this lady.

(Veronica grabs Amy's hand)

Don't touch me bitch!

(Amy pulls her hand from her Veronica and spits in her face)

You have a bitchy attitude just like your mother!

(Amy runs away)

Veronica yells at the officers to go after her!

(The officers run after Amy)

# When It Rains It Pours

This is a complete mess!

(Victoria begins to throw up and faints to the floor)

Sarah hovers over Victoria and asked her if she was okay. Lord help me! Shut up, Sarah, your God, can't help you now! Your daughter is going to prison. I don't care if she is sick. Shut up, Veronica, and call the ambulance; she is not breathing!

(The officer calls the ambulance and uncuffs Victoria)

(Veronica asked the officers if they found her granddaughter)

No, madam, we lost her. Do your fucking job and find my granddaughter before I make all of you lose your jobs! I will sue the predict! I can't believe this bullshit is happening!

(The ambulance arrives, and the paramedics put Victoria on a stretcher into the ambulance)

# When It Rains It Pours

Sarah goes with Victoria in the ambulance to the hospital. Lord help me! Please heal my daughter so she can live! Lord, please protect Amy and bring her back to us safely!

# Chapter Eight

## *A Blessing In Disguise*

The paramedics gave Victoria oxygen, and they were able to revive her in the ambulance. They took her to the hospital to examine her. When they arrived at the hospital, the nurses told Sarah she could not go into the emergency room. To her surprise, she saw Vernonia and Richard standing in the hospital lobby.

(Sarah looked at them in disgrace as she walked up to Richard)

Richard, you should be ashamed of yourself! Look at what you have done to Victoria and Amy. You ruined my family all because you wanted pussy! You blackmailed my daughter, and now she is on a hospital bed fighting for her life. Amy ran away, and no one can find her.

# A Blessing In Disguise

I don't know if she is still alive!

(Veronica speaks to Richard)

Richard, don't make Sarah talk to you like that! She must not know who we are! Demand respect from her now!

(Sarah starts to cry, and the doctor walks into the lobby)

Who is Victoria's mother? I am, sir! What is your name, madam? My name is Sarah Nelson. Nice to meet you, madam. I wanted to let you know we are examining your daughter, and we are running a blood test to find out the cause of her illness. Will she be okay, doctor? Yes, she should be! Doctor, please do whatever it takes to keep my daughter alive!

(The doctor walks away, and Sarah takes a seat)

Richard, what was Sarah talking about? Did you blackmail Victoria for pussy?

# A Blessing In Disguise

(Richard walks away from his mother)

Answer me, son! I am speaking to you! You have a mouth; use it! Don't talk to me like that, mother. I am a grown man! If you are a grown man, son, then answer my question! Did you blackmail Victoria for sex?

(Veronica slaps Richard across the face)

Answer me, boy! Yes, I slept with her once, and I blackmailed her to fuck me because I want her back! Are you happy now? I told you the truth, and now it's all my fault. What the fuck were you thinking, son? You are thinking with your dick instead of your head! You never learn, and I am tired of cleaning up your mess!

(At the moment Mark was leaving the hospital for his lunch break, and he saw Sarah crying in the lobby)

Hey Sarah, are you okay? Why are you crying? Hi Mark, you should have a seat.

# A Blessing In Disguise

Congratulations on your engagement! Thank you, but why are you crying? Victoria is in the emergency room, and Amy is missing; she ran away! What? My fiancé is in the emergency room! Where is Amy? I don't know where she is, and Victoria passed out!

(The doctor comes over to Sarah)

Madam, we have good news! What is it, doctor? Tell us this is my daughter's fiancé. Your daughter is pregnant. What? Thank you, Jesus, my daughter is okay!

(Mark hugged Sarah in excitement)

Are you serious, doctor? Yes! You can go into her room in the next 30 minutes to speak with her. Unfortunately, she is very weak right now. She has to stay overnight at the hospital for observation. She will be released tomorrow from the hospital to go home.

# A Blessing In Disguise

(Veronica and Richard look at each other in shock)

Did you hear that, son? Victoria is pregnant! Boy, you better hope she is not pregnant with your baby! You are a married man; what are you doing fucking Victoria? You have a beautiful wife at home! I am going to divorce my wife for Victoria. I am still in love with her! Are you crazy, boy? You will not divorce your wife for that whore! It all makes sense now you wanted me to press charges against her because she is engaged to Mark, and you are jealous. Boy, her pussy can't be that good for you not to use protection with her! Did you use protection, boy?

(Richard looks the other away, and Veronica slaps him across his face again)

Mom, stop hitting me. I am not a child!

# A Blessing In Disguise

Then answer me when I am speaking to you! No, I did not use protection! Boy, You are so stupid! I don't know what I am going to do with you!

(Veronica walks over to Sarah)

Sarah, you are lucky your daughter is pregnant! I have no other choice but to drop the charges. I hope she knows who is the father of her child! What is she talking about, Sarah? My son had sex with Victoria unprotected. He can be the father of the child! What? Are you serious?

(Richard walks over to Mark)

Yes, bitch ass, I fucked your fiancé! Now, what are you going to do about it? She wanted a black cock, and you could not satisfy her with your tiny pink dick! Richard, don't let my white coat foal you! I will fuck you up right here in this hospital! I will love to see you do it, Mark! I dare you to touch me!

# A Blessing In Disguise

(Mark takes off his white coat and swings at Richard as they began to fight in the hospital lobby)

The employees in the hospital yelled at the men to stop fighting!

(The security guards of the hospital ran over to break up the fight)

Richard took out a knife in his pocket and sliced Mark's face. I told you don't fuck with me, Mark! The security guards pulled them apart.

(Mark was bleeding all over his face, and the nurses rushed him into surgery)

Omg, Lord, can this day get any worse! Where is my granddaughter Amy?

(Veronica walks over to Sarah)

Your son-in-law got what he deserved, and tell him we are pressing charges against him for assaulting my son!

# A Blessing In Disguise

Where is Amy, Sarah? I don't know, Veronica! Richard, go find your daughter she is still missing!

(The doctor walks over to Sarah)

You can see your daughter now! Thank you, doctor!

(Sarah walks into Victoria hospital's room)

Hey baby, are you okay? I am feeling better, mom. I am so glad you are alive, Victoria. I thought I was going to lose you. God answered my prayers and brought you back to life. I am grateful for that. Where is Amy, mom? I don't know Victoria. I prayed, and I know God will protect her and bring her back to us safely. Do you know who the father of this child is? Unfortunately, I don't, mom! I had unprotected sex with Richard and Mark back to back. Omg, Victoria, you have to take a DNA test to find out who is the father of your unborn child. Mark knows you had sex with Richard. What? How does he know? Richard told him! What?

# A Blessing In Disguise

Yes, they got into a fight, and now Mark is in surgery. Richard sliced his face with a knife. Are you serious mom?

(Victoria's blood pressure went up, and she could not breathe)

The nurses quickly ran into the room. Victoria, are you okay?

(Victoria gaps for air)

Madam, you have to leave the room! You can't be in here right now!

(The nurses escort Sarah out of the room while they try to resuscitate her)

Sarah walks into the lobby with her head held down and prayed to God. Lord, I need your help right now! Heal my daughter! My daughter has to live to give birth to her unborn child. Amy has to return back home to us safely. Mark has to recover from his surgery. Lord, please help my family! Please answer my prayers quickly!

# Chapter Nine

*Who Is The Father Of The Child?*

(Shortly after Sarah finished her prayer, Amy walked into the hospital)

Amy, is that you? Yes, grandma! Thank you, God, for answering my prayer.

(Amy starts to cry)

Grandma, I am sorry I ran away. I did not want to leave with Veronica! I don't want to live with my father! I want to stay with you! I know, baby girl, I am here for you! I won't let Veronica or Richard take you away from me! Don't worry! God has our back! Are you okay, Amy? Yes, grandma! Where did you go? I went to a friend's house to hide from the police officers.

# Who Is The Father Of The Child?

Amy, how did you know I was here? I went back to your house, and the neighbors told me you went to the hospital with mommy. Is she okay? Yes, she is okay, baby girl; everything is in God's hands.

(The doctor walks over to Sarah)

Madam, Victoria has recovered from her high blood pressure, and she has requested that we perform a DNA test on two gentlemen. Are they here? Where is her fiancé? He is in surgery. Madam, is he okay? I believe he will be okay, doctor. Thanks for asking. Grandma, what happened to Mark? He got into an altercation, baby, but he will be okay. God is with him.

(Veronica & Richard walk into the hospital)

There she is, Richard! Where is she, mom? I don't see her. She is sitting next to Sarah. I told you Sarah knew where Amy was hiding the entire time. Son, don't trust that lady!

# Who Is The Father Of The Child?

(Veronica and Richard walk over to Amy)

Doctor, that young man walking towards us is one of the gentlemen that should be tested for the DNA test. Are you sure, madam, he is a married man? Yes, doctor, believe me, he has to be tested for a DNA test. Grandma, is mommy pregnant? Yes, baby girl! I am so happy for her, but why did you tell the doctor two men have to be tested for the DNA test. Baby girl, Richard or Mark, could be the father of Victoria's unborn child. What? Are you serious? Omg, that is disgusting; my mom slept with my dad.

I think I am going to vomit! Why would she do that? I thought she hated him. I can't believe she did it. Baby girl, she slept with him to keep full custody of you. Your father threatened your mother that he would take you away from her unless she had sex with him. What? Are you serious? I thought my father was married! Yes, he is, but he does not care. I feel so bad I judged my mother wrongfully.

# Who Is The Father Of The Child?

She will do anything for me, no matter what the outcome may be. My mother goes far and beyond to take care of me. I don't deserve to have a mother like her. I am ungrateful.

(Amy starts to cry)

Baby girl, don't cry. Victoria knows you love her. Be strong for your mother right now; she needs your support.

(The doctor walks over to Richard)

Young man, I was told you should be tested for a DNA test. You can be a father of an unborn child by Victoria Nelson. Yes, doctor, I had unprotected sex with her.

(Veronica interrupts their conversation)

Hi doctor, I am Veronica Richard's mom. Can I ask you a question? Yes, you can, madam. How many months pregnant is she? Madam, she is three months pregnant.

# Who Is The Father Of The Child?

Well, in that case, I am glad we came back to the hospital. My son needs to be tested! Doctor Victoria is a whore; she opens her legs for anyone. I doubt she knows who the father is.

(Veronica yells at Richard)

Boy, if you are the father of this child, you should be ashamed of yourself! I won't be ashamed, mom, because I am in love with Victoria.

(Veronica slaps Richard across the face)

Boy, are you dumb? Mom, stop hitting me. I am a grown man.

(The doctor interrupts their conversation)

I am sorry to interrupt but sir, please come with me for the DNA testing.

(Richard follows the doctor as Veronica walks over to Amy)

# Who Is The Father Of The Child?

Amy, where have you been? We have been looking all over for you! None of your business! I don't have to answer you! Yes, you do. I am your grandmother and soon-to-be guardian. You will do whatever I tell you too. Veronica, Amy is not going anywhere with you! She is staying here with me! Shut up, Sarah! Stop praying to your God; he is ruining my plans. Your daughter should be in prison locked up behind bars for the crimes she has committed. Victoria can't keep her legs closed, and she could be pregnant with my son's child again. Can this day get any worse! As a matter of fact, Sarah, you should pray for your daughter so she could stop selling her pussy for money.

(Amy stands up to Veronica)

Stop talking about my mother like that! You arrogant, self-righteous piece of shit!

(Veronica slaps Amy across the face, and Amy spits in her face)

# Who Is The Father Of The Child?

You disrespectful piece of shit, you will regret this! Didn't your mother teach you to respect your elders! Your mother should have listened to me when I told her to abort you! I wish you were never born because you and your mother ruined my son's life. He can't get over Victoria, and now he is willing to lose everything for your whoring ass mother.

(Richard walks back into the lobby towards his mother)

Did you get the results yet, son? Not yet, mom. I am patiently waiting.

(Richard approaches Amy)

Hi Amy, I am your father! It is a pleasure to finally meet you. I have been dreaming of this moment my entire life to see you face to face. Can I hug you?

(Richard opens his arms to hug Amy)

# Who Is The Father Of The Child?

Please don't touch me, Richard! Wow, you are feisty, just like your mother. I apologize for not being in your life, Amy, and I want to make it up to you. No, thank you, Richard. I am not interested in having a relationship with you! Son, this child is so disrespectful she should not be calling you by your name. Teach her manners, son, because clearly, her mother didn't. Shut up, bitch no one is talking to you! Wow, she has a mouth just like her mother too!

   (Veronica yells at Amy)

Amy, keep it up! I got your ass in the palm of my hands. I can ruin your life! Sweetheart, don't talk to your grandmother like that. Don't call me sweetheart either, Richard! Why are you so angry at me? You threatened my mother to have sex with you! How could you do that? Aren't you a married man?

(Mark walks into the lobby and overhears the argument between Amy and Richard)

# Who Is The Father Of The Child?

What kind of father are you? I don't know what you are talking about, sweetheart. Don't act stupid, Richard! You told my mom if she did not have sex with you. You will file for full custody of me. I have no respect for you, and I don't want to have any relationship with you! You are a piece of shit to me! Don't talk to me like that, Amy. I am your father; show me respect!

(Mark approaches Richard)

Are you serious? You threatened Victoria to have sex with you! Yes, I did, Mark! What are you going to do about it? Now that you have your stitches in your face. Do you want me to reopen them? Should we go for round two? So I can fuck you up again! Yes, let's go for round two, homeboy, so I can teach you how to be a man!

(Mark takes off his bandages and prepares to fight Richard)

# Who Is The Father Of The Child?

Amy yells, beat him up, Mark! Teach that piece of shit a lesson!

(Suddenly, the doctor walks into the lobby with the results, and everyone becomes quiet)

Gentlemen, I am glad I have you both here. I have the results from the DNA test. What are the results, doctor? I have good and bad news. I hate to be the bearer of bad news. Doctor, tell us! We need to know! Son, you better start praying before you lose everything! I don't care; mom shut up so I can hear the results.

(Veronica slaps Richard across the face and the doctor stops talking)

Stop hitting me, mom! Now is not the time to argue; please be quiet. Doctor, we apologize for the interpretation. Thank you, Richard!

# Who Is The Father Of The Child?

There is no easy way to say this because I know both of you are in love with Victoria, but only one of you can be the father. Doctor, the suspense is killing me; please tell us already! According to my test results, the father of the child is the man Victoria truly loves.

## TO BE CONTINUED...

# Books By The Author

To Love or To Hate: Book One

To Love or To Hate: Book Two

Predestined To Be

Lilly Loves the Flowers of Spring

Amy's Birthday Wish

Do Not Cry Black Lives Matter

# Books By The Author

Glambitious: Guide to Self-Love Confidence & Happiness eBook

Win While You Wait: How to Prosper During The Process eBook

Birth Your Book In 5 Days eBook

The Book Marketing Guide eBook

How To Make $5k In 30 Days eBook

# About The Author

In all of Ashleigh Henry's accomplishments, and her endeavors. She sees herself in the future as an overcomer and a mountain mover. She is overcoming every obstacle that comes her way with Jesus Christ in her life, directing her path. She sets her standards high because she knows she must achieve nothing but the best. She often reflects on her mom's struggles to pay her tuition to send her to a private school. Her mom made sure she had the best education she never had. Ashleigh knows she has a purpose and a destiny to accomplish. She knows who and what she wants to become. When I think of Ashleigh I dream and only can imagine great things.

For more information or to get in touch with Ashleigh, please visit www.iamashleighhenry.com

www.ingramcontent.com/pod-product-compliance
Lightning Source LLC
Chambersburg PA
CBHW071833290426
44109CB00017B/1815